M000315603

COMING OUT
OF THE
Shell

Living with HIV, Schizophrenia, Lichen Planus, Migraines, and Obesity

MARLYN TORRES

ISBN 978-1-0980-4118-2 (paperback)
ISBN 978-1-0980-4119-9 (digital)

Christian Faith Publishing, Inc.
832 Park Avenue
Meadville, PA 16335
www.christianfaithpublishing.com

Printed in the United States of America

CONTENTS

ACKNOWLEDGMENTS

As I was meditating as to whom I will dedicate this book, it came to my mind my mother to whom I have so much respect for her love and dedication that she has had for all her children. She is a woman of faith whom life has treated very harshly, but with God's help, she is still standing.

I honor Mom for being there for me in my ups and downs in this crazy life. I love you, and I hope we have many more years to spend together with the blessings of the Lord by our side. So I dedicate this book to you, Mami, and I wish you many more years of life in health and vitality.

I want to thank my good friends that have been with me all these years of confusion for being patient, for showing me love and understanding even though I didn't have a clue of what was going on in my life, especially Amanda who choose to stick with me for twenty-four years.

Maria, Leida, Tere, and Alina, I just want to tell you thank you publicly.

And I can't finish without thanking all the men of God that have taught me the Word of God. Thank you for implanting the Word in my heart that made me stronger on my faith.

I also want to thank my son for having patience with me and for understanding me and for being kind with my brother through all his crisis and also for honoring my mom and helping her in all he can to make her life a little bit more easy. I love you, Ricky.

And last but not least, I want to thank God for allowing me to write this book which, I think, is going to be a blessing to you all.

INTRODUCTION

Most of you who pick this book will turn the pages for answer of some things that relate with you. You might be curious and ask yourself, "What is she going to offer to me with her testimony?"

Well, I wrote this book to everyone that wants a deeper understanding of the pain and deliverance of my own struggles in my walk with these diseases and the awesome privilege to have the presence of the Lord walking with me all these years.

I want to share with you a blessing about His wonders, dreams, and, most importantly, the call of God for you.

"Yea, though I walk through the valley of shadow of death, I will fear no evil: for thou art with me; thy rod and staff they comfort me" (Psalm 23:4).

Who would imagine that I will be chosen by the Almighty God to speak to you?

My Blessings to You

I pray to the Lord of Hosts to bless you as you read this blessing. May the Lord release the presence of the Holy Spirit and touch you in a powerful way that the anointing that destroy yokes will be upon you in every area your life.

I pray that God will help you to experience a glimpse of His glory and that the power of God will be manifested in you today.

Lord, I pray that if there is anyone who is sick, you will heal them and bring to their lives restoration not only physically but spiritually as well. Jesus, touch them through the power of Your Holy Spirit and release Your power upon them.

I ask You that as a consequence of reading this book, they will have an encounter with You, Lord Jesus, and that their eyes will be enlightened with Your Word. I pray that they will find hope and that You will restore their family with the knowledge of our Lord Jesus Christ. In Your precious name, I pray. Amen.

Coming Out of the Shell

This title is of special significance to me. It means new birth. To me, it means exposure to a new beginning. Let's take a hen as an example. When it has the eggs, they go through a process before it becomes chicks. They need to be heated under the wings of the hen before the shell begins to crack, then they come out of the shell. And boom! The chick comes to existence.

The same thing happened to me. While I was covered by the shell, I had faced fear asking myself, When will I die? I faced betrayal, rejection, and lots of moment while my mind wasn't sure what to do next. Now I don't care what others might think about me. And my purpose is to help you understand that the only One that really cares is God.

With all the pain that these illnesses or diseases have brought to my life, I can certainly say that *I'm still standing* after thirty years of HIV, twenty-one of schizophrenia, like five of lichen planus, plus you can add migraines and obesity. But the true reason of my victory while dealing with all these issues is that I have been declaring that by Jesus's stripes, I am healed. This walk of faith has been tough because, at times, I felt crazy or with pain; but no matter how I felt, I kept proclaiming the Word of God that brings victory.

I don't know when I'm going to die, or if they will discover the vaccine for HIV/AIDS; but one thing I know is that I have a tremendous promise from God, and that is that if I believe in Jesus, He promised me that I will be in heaven with Him. It brings me great comfort that I have been able to believe in Jesus.

I want to tell you that you are not alone, and whatever circumstance you are facing right now, let me tell you that there is always hope. Why hope? Because if you choose to believe in Jesus, you will have everlasting life and you have the option to confess healing by the stripes of Jesus. Once the decision is made, you won't be so worried if you live or die because you have a better promise, and of course, nobody wants to die. But you will live your life with security of having this comfort in your life.

The protection of the Lord will be upon your life, and you can begin to entrust the Lord in all your affairs. You can also come out of the shell and tell the world that Jesus is real and that He has saved you and that you have put your trust in Him for your salvation and healing. Because that is what this is all about: telling others about Jesus.

This idea of writing a book was in my mind since I suffered the crisis with schizophrenia but was never able to accomplish my dream. But now that I have this goal, it will be accomplished with God's help. I decide that I want to share with the world the goodness of God and how He has kept me throughout all these years with HIV without being sick in the hospital.

So, as I always speak to myself, I say to myself, "Marlyn, come out of the shell." There is a bright future for you no matter what you are facing right now. God is bigger, and a new episode is ready to explode for you. I believe there will be people who are going to be encouraged, and their faith is going to grow stronger. I believe that as a consequence of this book, people are going to contact me to share my testimony and be able to minister the Word of God and that miracles are going to happen. Why? Because I serve a living God that never gets late to meet me wherever I am. So Marlyn, now it's your time to shine and succeed in all you do. So, let's begin from this day forward, and Marlyn, come out of the shell.

Story of My Life

Beloved reader, I'm going to start with a verse that is found in Psalm 139:13: "For you form my inward parts; you covered me in my mother's womb." Why did I start with this verse? Growing up as a child, I was told that my father used to hit my mom's belly to prevent me to come to this world. But the Lord was faithful to guard me even in my mother's womb.

As a little girl, I didn't have a father figure in my life due to a divorce in my early stages of life. But even though I was told that my father didn't want me, I always had the need of him in my life. He died when I was seven, and the fact that he left me seven thousand dollars kind of comforted me. When I was in school, I felt jealous of my friends that were picked up by their parents. And later on, I realized that money didn't matter.

I'm the only girl in the family of four. My mom got a second separation after her first divorce, and everything was very dysfunctional in the family. She was a nurse and always left us with our grandmother. When I was around eight, my grandmother died, but she left a seed of God into our lives. Then my mom had to stop working and took care of us the best she could. But in the three of us was the need of the father figure. When we became teenager, we began to go to parties and stay late at night outside of the house. As a consequence of a crazy life, we lost our brother. He hung himself in a tree in front of our house. That was a very traumatic experience for all of us.

Then I went to college but couldn't finish. Then my crazy life started going to parties here and there, having a promiscuous life, and there, I met my first husband. My mom made me marry him because she thought he was the first one, but what she didn't know was that I started to have sex long way before. He was nice enough to marry me, but there wasn't love; it was just attraction. I was eighteen when that happened, so I believe it gave me HIV.

I'm not sure if he did because I never confronted him, but based on his drug history, that's what I guess. I only lived with him for three months, and by the sixth month of marriage, I was divorced. Then I got curious to come to New Jersey, and I did. Here, I met my second husband, and he lied to me and told me that he was divorced; but it wasn't the truth. I was so naïve at nineteen years old. I just wanted affection, so I believed him and moved in with him. He finally got divorced but had four children before me. I had two boys with him and having the other ones who weren't mine on the weekends makes me grow up a little bit faster. I don't know if I truly loved him or it just was some way to void the need I had.

In 1994, I met the Lord as my personal Savior, and I began to straighten everything out. I married him because I wanted to be right with the Lord.

As a couple, we wanted to be close to our families in Puerto Rico, and he bought the piece of land where my mom was living, so we began to build a house there. But we needed money, so we decided to leave the two boys with my mom and work hard to finish the house. But a few months after, my first son got sick of pneumonia and got hospitalized. I receive a phone call from my mom telling that I had to go to PR immediately, so I did. The doctor was straight to the point. He told me that he had AIDS and that he will die in a few months. I didn't even know what that was. He told all the family to get tested. My youngest son was negative, and my ex was negative. I was positive. He died in May 1995 at the children's hospital in Newark, New Jersey. They let me hold him dead in my hands. Just to remember it brings tears to my eyes. Then after that, my life never was the same.

My ex started to blame me for the death of my son, and both pains make me lose interest in him. Finally, I left him. I found myself raising a child in the projects in Elizabeth, New Jersey, living from the system and paying back all the money that I took when I was lying with his father. It wasn't easy to raise a child that was HIV negative and me being positive. Back then, there was very few knowledge about the virus, and they were telling me that I had to wash everything with Clorox. I was so nervous and afraid.

My first home church was Presbyterian, and I really learned a lot about the Lord. I was so hungry that I didn't miss a Bible study. Sometimes it was like four or five people, but I was there. I was so much in pain just to know that I was going to die, and the loss of my son made me wonder if I will see my son growing up to teenage life. Tears run through my eyes every time I went to doctor's appointments seeing all those people that was in their last stage of life. My son was four years old and didn't have a clue of what was going on about everything. He just looked forward to every visit because they will treat him with ensure, and he loved it. He was looking forward for it in every visit, but I wasn't because every time, it will bring me close to the reality of death.

I was deeply saddened and depressed for the loss of my son and my status. Then I began to miss church and was hearing voices. I got completely crazy, out of mind. My ex used to take my son every weekend for visits, and I was so sick that I got hospitalized. They diagnosed me with schizophrenia. I got discharged, but one week later, I went back in. I was so sick that after the meds they put on, I was walking like a robot. And after that, my life was never the same. It's been a journey. I really don't know how I raised my son. I have been so sick through all these years.

Living a life as a single mom with HIV, I went through lots of rejections, fears, and tears. Many times, I felt so lonely, unwanted even though I'm beautiful. I made lots of wrong choices. When I was introduced to the internet, I used to spend hours talking nonsense, and I had a few blind dates, of course. I always told them I'm HIV positive, but my focus was to fill a void. Even though the Lord was always there, I wanted to do what I wanted and didn't care too much. I guess I didn't have a revelation of who He is.

When my son was fourteen or fifteen, my oldest brother was missing, and it broke our hearts. I decided to move to Puerto Rico. I stayed there for one year, but my life didn't have meaning there because before I was volunteering at the relief bus, which is an organization that feeds homeless. I volunteered there a few years before I left for Puerto Rico, so it was something meaningful I was doing and with purpose. So, I came back and I got back on my feet and got my apartment alone because my son decided to stay in Puerto Rico with his father.

Here, I met my third husband. He was from New York. So, after I became stable in New Jersey, I decided to leave everything for him. What a mistake and what a not-mistake because the Word says in Roman 8:28 that everything works for our good when we are in Christ Jesus. It was a big change, but don't forget, I was still schizophrenic. I managed with the schizophrenia. I wasn't hearing voices, but still, my thought life was challenging.

I was able to have a job and maintain it for five years. But my marriage only lasted four years due to the fact that he was an alcoholic and had a very bad temper. He verbally abused me and manipulated me like he wished. As a consequence of that experience, my walk with the Lord grew stronger, and I decided not to seek anymore for affection on the internet. I learned my lesson, and I realized that the only One that loves me without conditions is the Lord Jesus Christ. Then I left him for sure.

I ended up in a shelter. The night that I left him, he was extremely drunk and abusive, but thank God it was only for one night. But I got the taste of how bad it is to be in a shelter. So I know what many people that live in shelters feel. Then I went to live in rooms. I went to two different rooms with man drinking and loud music. Then I found a studio; it was a box but at least had kitchen and bathroom on its own, and I was grateful with that. Now I'm living in a bigger apartment but still struggle with financial circumstances.

After I left my husband, I found myself without a job. I tried to apply for disability, but they didn't approve it. So, I decided to work as nanny, but I always battle within myself about my status, so I lost my job because I revealed it. Now I am in that situation, and I said, "Why not share my story with the world and be able to be a blessing to all of those that have been in my place and to inform all those that are having sex without control without realizing that the consequences that it will bring?" It will bring tears, lost, rejection, and death.

Thanks to the Father, to the Son, and to the Holy Spirit for being faithful to me when I wasn't and to be able to put up with me all this years. I just want to tell the world the blessing that has been for me to have the Lord through all these years. He has been the only One that understood me when I was in my darkest hours. He has held my tears and helped me all the way through. So, this is a glimpse of what my life has been, so thank you, God. And I hope you can see with a better view how far God has taken me through for almost thirty years.

Beginning of a New Life

After all these things that have happened to me, I chose to start again. Every day we have new opportunities to begin again. Today I choose to trust the Lord, love Him, and serve Him with all my heart. There was a day when I decided to begin in the walk of God's kingdom, and in that walk that I chose, my life has been transformed with ups and downs but never went back. Maybe you did and fell away from that new life that you were supposed to begin with Him, but let me tell you, my beloved reader, there is always an opportunity that God gives us every day. It's never too late to make a decision for Jesus.

Beginning again, what does it mean? It means new opportunities to start something new. It could be at your work, home with children, at the gym, which I'm guilty off, lol. But no matter what, there will be a new day to start again.

When we give our lives to Jesus, recognizing that He is the only One that can clean all the mess that our lives brought us too, we can start a brand-new life, and all sins are forgiven. And we have the opportunity to start a new life, not only because that decision will bring physical changes but also spiritual as well.

So, what that decision does to our lives, it brings joy, peace, and a new sense of freedom that helps us to rest knowing that all that matters is Jesus. When we begin to experience the power of the Holy Spirit helping us to start a brand-new walk with the Lord, we will be amazed of how the Holy Spirit will give you revelation of His Word and help you to connect with the Father in ways you never expected.

The children of Israel began a new walk with the Lord when they were released from slavery, but they had a heart of complaining and wanted to go back. They had all the provision that God had store for them, but they didn't appreciate it. God's purpose was to bless them with a land that flows milk and honey, but they were unsatisfied. They cursed the very blessing that God has for them. All that God wanted was to bless His people, and when they started complaining, they stopped that which was meant for them. Because God's purpose is to bless His people, we have to be very careful not to want to go back. They were in the desert forty years when they could be there in a short period of time, and the older people didn't have the chance to enter the Promised Land. Just the new generation did.

So, we can decide what we are going to do in that process—whether to complain of the very blessing that God had given us or to embrace it with contentment and acceptance knowing that God has the best in store for us. Romans 8:28 says, "All things work for Good to those that are in Christ Jesus."

Every day I thank God for a brand-new day and for keeping me alive to be able to breathe and not take it for granted, to be able to smell a flower, and just to meditate in the awesome miracle of the humanity of how we all were formed in our mother's womb, and we all have the same things but unique in our own personalities. How God gives wisdom to mankind to build and to go to the moon and to create new medicines for our own benefit. So, praise be to God for a new day of opportunities that He allows us to have today.

In 1994, I had the awesome and wonderful opportunity to give my life to the Lord, and it was a life-changing experience to me until this day. I remember I was mopping my apartment and listening to a Christian radio station when I broke down in tears and gave my life to the King of kings and Lord of lords. This awesome privilege that He granted to me gave me more strength, peace, and joy. I never thought how wonderful it is just to experience His presence and to realize that the God of the universe loves me. I never knew that before until a few years ago that I got into that revelation. I learned to wait on Him and to respect myself, knowing that the only thing I need is Him. Thank You, Jesus, for giving me an opportunity to start again.

And you can start a brand-new life with Him if you choose it—recognizing the awesome privilege to have the Maker of the universe loving you and by your side.

Sickness and Disease that I Have to Deal With

There are five different things I have been dealing with: 1.) HIV 2.) Schizophrenia 3.) Lichen planus 4.) Obesity and 5.) Migraines, and none of them has stopped me from loving the Lord.

Each one of these I have had to treat them in different ways, and all have been a big challenge in my life. First I want to tell you, beloved reader, that I understand everyone that are dealing with any of these diseases or illnesses and that I'm going to talk from my heart and my experiences from different kind of people that have been there to judge and not to have a heart of understanding toward these medical issues and also how I dealt with it. Let's see how I dealt with every single one of them.

HIV

It's a simple virus that is in your blood. The only ways you can get infected is through unprotected sex or from blood to blood, not by tears or sweat or urine or by physical touch. I have experienced so much rejection through all these years. I had a lady that when I told her, she was afraid to give a kiss on my cheek or to touch me. Finally, I got rid of her; the other one stopped talking to me like I was a rare thing. When I told my friends, I was afraid to even eat in their house because I didn't know how they will approach me with the utensils or plates.

In my early days, I was even afraid to go to have a manicure, and even if I tell them, they will be even more afraid than to have the work done. I was afraid of what others will say or do; it kept me from enjoying life to the fullness. One of my biggest mistakes was to believe that I was the only one that was going through that, but then

16

I realized anyone could have it and might not know that they have the disease. I got infected through sex, and there are others that have been by drug abuse or a transfusion; but no matter how we got it, I just want to tell the world that we are human beings and that we get hurt by your rejection.

We need more love and compassion than ever before because we have loved ones that are suffering just to know about our disease. Some of us have lost loved ones, and those scars are there. Some of us have kept our status to our self and have fear of what others will say or do. So, I just plead to the world to be compassionate like Jesus had when He healed the sick and the oppressed. Compassion, comprehension, and love—these are what we all need. And how I have treated HIV? By taking my meds every day and live life like I don't have anything.

Schizophrenia

To deal with a mental illness is not easy. When you have an imbalance in your brain, it could be very difficult. You don't have the ability to process your thoughts like a normal person. Sometimes as a consequence of the disease, you can hear voices or have paranoia thinking that everyone is following you. I did have that. I thought that everyone knew what I was thinking or hallucinating. Even something I experienced were sensations in my body that were very uncomfortable, and 'til this day, I still take medications for it.

Sometimes people with mental illness are very smart or talented. My brother suffers the same as me, and he is an artist. He has sold many paintings and ceramics that he did on his own disease. When someone suffers from schizophrenia, they have to be under supervision unless they are stable like me. My brother in one crisis, he nailed his eyes, and as a consequence, he lost one eye.

So you see, sometimes people are quick to judge because their appearance might be a little out of the normal, or their actions are weird; but what they don't realize is that either are an imbalance or spiritual forces that are attacking the people that are bound in this area of their lives.

We need understanding and patience. Sometimes we might say things or do things that are out of control, but what they don't know is that we might be thinking in a schizophrenic stage without realizing that we are doing that being sick. I just want to encourage you that are having any mental illness not to suffer it alone. Find someone to talk to. Go to the park, relax, express your feelings, and find something to do if you can have a part-time job or go to therapy. Take out of your life all that people that speak negative to your life or who don't value you.

For me, it's been a tremendous help to have the Lord in my life. I tell Him everything knowing that He won't judge me but understand every crazy thought that I have because He made me and loves me. We need love and understanding, someone we can talk about our struggles with, and mostly, we need the Lord to help us to overcome every thought that comes our way. I treat schizophrenia trying to understand my life and study my reactions, trying to control my thoughts even though sometimes, it comes automatically. As I study more about the mind, I found out I'm not as crazy the doctors think.

Lichen planus

It's amazing I can't still comprehend the severity of this condition. I began to have a severe rash or spots in legs and wrist it was itchy, and it stayed for around one year and a half. I couldn't deal with it anymore, and I heard a message from my pastor talking about that we have power in what we speak over our lives, over our finances, over our family, and over ourselves.

When God created the world, He spoke. He didn't take time to make everything, but He spoke, and it was done. And there is a passage in Mark 11: 12–14 when Jesus cursed the fig tree, so in our lives, we have the power to curse every disease that comes our way. It was a very uncomfortable situation to have this itchy and spreading rash, so I grabbed hold of the Word of God, and I cursed lichen planus every day; and all of a sudden, it went away. I treated it like this. I said every day that every cell of lichen planus in my life will dry up from its root because I am healed by His stripes. And it did. Praise be to Jesus.

Obesity

Oh, my goodness. After the death of my son, I got into a big depression. All I wanted to do was eat and sleep. I spent my life doing like that for more than ten years, and it's not that I have overcome it. For me, I get anxious when I have something that bothers me, and I eat. I know I should do some exercise, but I'm lazy, and I lack the motivation to do it. I wish I have the money to eat only healthy food, but you know, every place you go there are cakes and potatoes chips. And can you imagine if I am in one of my bad days? What I do is I eat them.

Obesity is something that I need to overcome as well as the other things I did. I know that there are some consequences if I don't take action, like diabetes, heart disease, or fatigue. For me, being overweight is a challenging topic. I believe in myself, but I need God's help to be able to say no and overcome all the unhealthy food and to live a long and healthy life—and right now I'm trying to eat more healthy and exercise a little bit more.

Migraines

Wow, this was very bad. When I was going through my divorce, I began to suffer very bad migraines. It wasn't something that will stay for hours, but it was a strong pain in my front head and back head that will take all my strength away. My legs will get numb, I had nausea, and I see flashes. And a few times, I had to go to the emergency room. I was afraid to drive. I was afraid to go to the supermarket because the smells will give me migraine. I also had to ask the doctor to give me a note for my job because I couldn't drive. I was also afraid to eat certain food. Well, it was horrible.

In winter last year, I began to take vitamins and fish oil every day and thank God it has decreased this year. So, this is just a glimpse of what I have been through with the physical challenges that I had. I hope you will be blessed with what you just have read, and hopefully one day, you will see me with like sixty pounds less.

Some Experiences about Schizophrenia

How do I start this? It's difficult to dig in something so complicated like my mind. I know you all like movies and things that has to do with spiritual world, but one thing is movies, and another thing is to live it day by day with thought that gets so deep inside of you that you don't even comprehend what is real or not. Confusion was a part of my daily living and not only confusion but paranoia as well, thinking that everybody knew my thoughts and what my next move will be. But let me start from the beginning, so you can have a glimpse of what I dealt with even though some thoughts have gone away but still are part of my world.

All started soon after my son's death. I began to hear voices, but I thought it was normal because I have never experienced that. So, I went with the flow; the voices will come on and off. And there start that spiritual world in my mind. My personal life was a mess, and an intense pain was deep within my soul. The pain to be accused of the death of my son made it worse. So, one day I decide that it was enough of pain for me, and I took my son and left my husband without realizing that I was making things worse. Then you add to it the stress to have to go to the court to see who my other son will be with. The voices became more real to me, and one day I found myself doing what the voices were telling me to do without knowing I was into a very bad crisis.

I remember it was on a weekend. My son used to go with his father on weekends, and I got completely crazy. I was ironing my son's clothes, so he could go on the weekend with his dad, and I could feel the spirits coming out of his clothes. I began to tear all the cloths that has flowers on it and made a pile of cloth on the floor. I was cleaning spirits that I could see on walls. I broke the fish tank, the TV, the ID caller, and the mirror. Everything was pretty destroyed. I was fasting, trying to cleanse myself from evil spirits and drinking olive oil because it represents the Holy Spirit.

And I was breaking the curses that all the world was making against me because I was representing the God. For me, the world will end in three days. Then I began to hear millions of voices from hell saying, "Lord, have mercy all in one accord." To this day, I remember those voices as clear as that day. In my attempt to completely cleanse myself, I began to dress in white. It was a complete battle in my mind among cleaning spirits, hearing voices, and breaking curses. It was a constant battle in my mind. So, I got to the point that I ran out of olive oil, so I decided to go to my part-time job that I had in a jewelry store and asked for my pay for the week.

They immediately knew something was wrong with me, dressed all in white, and with sandals on my feet, speaking in thongs which I never did before. So, they finally paid me, and I drove to the super-market to get my olive oil but, remember, still breaking curses and seeing spirits on everything I see, so I was removing labels from the items on the aisles. And because all my papers had finished, I began to tear my money and tossing it through the aisles. It happened to be that my pastor was on that supermarket that day, and he saw me. He said hi but noticed something was wrong, so he followed me in the supermarket and saw me breaking the money and tossing it through the aisles but didn't approach me. That day finally, I got the olive oil and drove back breaking curses in my mind. And as I was driving, I could literally see the angels of the Lord stopping my car in every light or stop sign. Finally, I got home, drank the olive oil, and con-tinued to clean the hallway from evil spirits. I didn't sleep the whole night. I was on a mission because the world will end soon.

So, the next day, I was burning my meds and plants while clean-ing the spirits on the hallway, and all of a sudden, I see my pastor with the whole congregation that came to visit me. I said hi to them but didn't receive them because I thought they were messengers of Satan. And they instantly knew something was wrong with me, then they saw the smoke coming out of my window. They immediately called the fire department, and in one minute, my apartment was filled with police, paramedics, fire department, and an ambulance. I remember telling the police that they cannot break the rules. So, I spoke in tongues all the way to the hospital, and my mind was completely gone. So, they left me on the observation room, and the nurses got distracted while I was cleansing the spirits from the wall that I ripped the wall up and destroyed it.

They immediately admitted me into the hospital. I didn't want to take the meds, and they restrained me with leather belts and injected me with the medicine; but to me, it was the spirits. So, I didn't want to eat anything. In my attempt to dress in white, I put a blanket around my neck, and they thought that I was trying to commit suicide. So, they put me in a very small room without lights with one mattress on the floor, and I began to cry and to spit all over and vomited. I remember myself sitting on the floor crying and screaming to them to take me out of there. I grabbed my knees on the floor crying, and just by the grace of God, they took me out. Then I began to hallucinate. I saw a snake coming out of the mouth of one of the patients. For me, he was the devil, and I got scared and told the nurses that he was bothering me, so they kept me in my bedroom.

I sneaked in a very small Bible the size of a keychain, and I was trying to read it but still breaking curses. Then I began to feel a little bit better, and it happened that the next day, a pastor was visiting patients, and he spoke to me. Now I realize that that was an angel by the Lord to comfort me and to let me know that I wasn't alone. I begged him to leave me his Bible, and he did.

In my craziness and spiritual state of mind, I began to clean the Bible with napkins with a little water and wiped it very well because it was holy to me. While I was in the battle, I was surrounded by God's protection even in my difficult situation. So, I began to get better, and I got released. To this day, I don't know how long I stayed admitted in that hospital. But thank God for good friends. One of my best friends picked me up. She wanted to take a taxi, but I didn't let her, so we walked all the way back home. I remember walking like a robot with all the medications. They put me on. I couldn't speak clearly, and I was stiff.

So, I got home with all kinds of emotions and feelings because I was feeling a weird sensation in my body. I remember that that sensation was very uncomfortable. And to my surprise, I found candles behind the door and a bowl with water and eggs underneath my bed. They said that it was supposed to help me, and guess who put that there? My ex. When he was back to return my son to me, I took the eggs and threw it at him, breaking it on his legs, and I said all kind of things to him. My mom has come from PR to take care of me, and I wasn't completely healed. So, I was trying to rest but still sick. Then I remember that my son ran out of milk, and there were some teenagers playing around with a glove with scissors, and I began to tell them that they were from the devil. When I came back home, I took the nail polish and a hammer. I popped them all in the kitchen at night.

My mom was fixing a blouse in the bed, and I started to feel the sensations in my body, and I took the blouse. I threw it at her telling her that she was the devil. She got scared of me and called my friend, and they decided to call the ambulance. So, I got admitted again. Until this day, I don't know how long I was there. I still didn't want to eat certain foods. I asked my mom to bring frozen fruits to me, and every time she visited me, she brought it. I got better and got released. Then nurses will visit me like three times a week to make sure I was taking my meds. So, it happened that as time passed by, and my mom had to leave to PR, and I began to raise my son alone with the help of nurses and friends. I reintegrated to my church family and began a new life; still sick but more stable. The voices began to disappear, and I began to feel a little bit better.

I was recovering day by day. One day I decided to look for a job, and I answered an ad in the newspaper. I found the place a little weird but still with the desire to work. It wasn't a big company. The building was dirty, and it was only a few people having a training. They told me that if I worked hard, I will be a millionaire, so I decided that I was going to work hard. The job was going from house to house, trying to sell vacuum cleaners and to give demonstrations in different houses. I barely ate and worked late at night. When the time came to be paid, they gave me a check that bounced. I told them, and they told me to deposit it again, and it bounced again. So, I left without being paid with lots of bounced checks and not only that. I spent the gas and tolls; it was a mess.

Then the schizophrenia turned 360 degrees from cleaning spirits to believing that millionaire people were controlling my life. So, I never went back to work and raised my son breaking curses and paranoiac thinking that these millionaire people were watching my life. I remember every time I saw my son touching his face and another person touch his face at the same time. I would tell my son, "Why are you making signs to that person?" Until this day, I think in the possibility that it will be real that they are in some type of control of my life and that there is a battle between good and evil, and it really affected my way of thinking.

Being Christians, we believe that there are two forces in this world. And we know that there are two kingdoms, the kingdom of God and the kingdom of darkness. So, I still break curses but, in another way, as I feel led by the Lord, and there are days that I can't control my mind, and my mind gets a little bit out of control with these two worlds. But immediately, I bowed my knees to God and asked for help, and all my fears and confusions, I surrendered them to Him. And when I get up from that floor, I feel renewed and afresh to start a new day. You don't know how many tears I have cried to the Lord in my confusion.

So now I rely on the Holy Spirit to direct my steps, and with Him, I know I have conquered as Jesus did. So, my final thoughts to you that are suffering from schizophrenia or depression are:

Life is the way you see it. You can overcome any thoughts that come your way. If you learn to rely on the Father, He will take you out of any situation. He wants to help you in your confusion, but you have to leave Him to direct your steps, and I promise you that He will work wonders in your life. He has helped me to overcome day by day. And believe me, He has been faithful. He loves you unconditionally. He knows everything about you, your thoughts, tears, and frustration. He knows your life better than you know yourself. He is compassionate toward you and wants to help you. Just surrender every thought, your emotions, and your problems. He wants to heal your mind and give you the opportunity to rest in His arms. He wants to lavish you with good health and demonstrate His power in your life. So, I encourage you to just believe in Him, and He will do wonders in your life as He has done in my life. Although I'm still with some challenges but only the Lord knows when it will go away. But one thing I can tell you, and that is that my life has changed completely when I learned to surrender to Him, the only One that truly loves me and truly loves you. He is your Father and knows everything about you. So, say yes to Him, and your life will be transformed. I hope you can identify with my experience.

If you are struggling with any mental illness, I pray that you will find hope in the only One that can turn your life around.

Fear of Death

When I discovered that my son was going to die and that I will, too, eventually, a big sense of fear grabbed hold of me. I used to cry and cry knowing that my son will pass away; I was afraid to let others know what was going on with him, and when they asked me why he passed away, I didn't know what to say because everybody was afraid of AIDS. Until this day, people don't get educated about AIDS or HIV, and they have so many misconceptions of how they could get infected…

Not only do I have fear of death because I have a disease like this one but there are many other diseases that can bring me to death, and that brought a great fear to my life. Often people are afraid of dying in an airplane crash or an automobile accident. Fear of death is something that is common in humans, but the reality of life is that one day, we were born and one day we are going to die.

We have to see how we can get rid of fear.

Well, the Bible says 1 John 4:18: "There is no fear in Love; but perfect Love cast out fear, because fear involves torment. But he who fears has not been made perfect in love."

Fear involves torment and we want to live a life full of Peace and Joy in the Lord and if the Love of God is inside of us, we ought to be secure in him knowing that everything is in his hands. And trusting the Lord is the only way that we can get rid of fear…that's the only way my beloved reader.

The Word of God says in 1 John 4:19 that we love HIM because he first loved us. So, if we know that He loved us first we should be secure in HIM knowing that all fear should be out of our lives because we have HIM

Look what Romans 8:39 says that "if God is for us who can be against us? And it goes on and tell us in verse 38 "For I am persuaded that neither death nor life, nor angels nor principalities, nor powers, nor things present nor things to come, nor height nor depth nor any created thing, shall be able to separate us from the Love of God which is in Christ Jesus our Lord...

So, you see, beloved reader, we don't have to be afraid of death because nothing shall be able to separate us from the love of God...

Even Jesus had to face death, and as a human, he sweat drops of blood knowing the pain of separation and the sin of all humankind that he had upon his shoulders. But he was secure in God, trusting Him that everything will be okay. He said when He was back to die, "Father in Thy hands, I commit my spirit, fully trusting the Father that He will make a way," even though he felt abandoned.

When we begin to trust God with our future and are sure that our lives are hidden in Jesus no matter what comes our way, we are secure in Him, who knows the length of our days. The Word of God says in James 4:14, "For your life is like the morning fog—it is here a little while, then it is gone."

Only the Lord knows when we are going to die, not the doctors, not the psychics, but the Lord. He is the maker of all, and in Him we exist and live. So why fear of death? Leave your life in God's hands and everything is going to be all right.

Healing from the
Inside Out

All these years of dealing with HIV and a mental illness, I realize that the more connected I am to the Lord, the more I begin to experience healing. I know it's a tough topic. How would a person that has been dealing with all kinds of issues could still believe the Lord for healing?

When I became a Christian, I used to ask God the question that many people that are in my same boat will. The question was, "Why, Lord, if You knew I was going to serve You? Why did you allow this to happen to me? Why, Lord? Is it because you don't love me?" But after I began to mature in Him, I realize that it's not the Lord that put this illness in my life. It's just a consequence of sin or that my body is subject to illnesses that come our ways.

When I realize that, I began to trust the Lord with all my might and confess the Word over my life, and if I tell you that I did every day through all these years, I will be a liar. But every now and then,

I grab hold of the Word of God that says in Isaiah 53:5 that by His stripes, we are healed.

One of the most important thing that we can do is to *trust him* in our daily living for healing and physical strength, but all begins with a relationship with Him. How can you trust someone that you don't know? That's why in this book, I made a lot of effort to make sure you begin a new life with Him because once you know that He loves you with an eternal love, you can be assure that He has your back in any circumstances in your life.

Once you know that the plans He has for you is to prosper you and that you be in good health (3 John 1:2), you begin to uncover the pages of your life and begin to see where He is trying to take you. He wants you to be in good health, and when you become to be familiar with His Word, things will start to change in your life. And believe me, it will be for your good.

When you love someone, you want that person to know it and experience good things in life. Let's see our love for our children. We want the best for them. The Word of God says in Matthew 7:11 that we being bad wants to give good things to our children. How much our heavenly Father to us? He is our Father and believe it or not, His plans are all the time good for us.

So why is this topic healing from the inside out? Because the best healing that a person needs to begin with is healing spiritually, and then the physical will start to manifest. I know it sounds a little difficult to believe, but believe me, as more close I am to Him, the more health I experience. Numbers 23:19 says that "He is not a man that would lie or a son of man that won't make it come through in your life." So just abandon yourself in the arms of our Father, and He will make sure you feel loved and cared for.

In my case, I have had to deal with all these diseases, but no matter what, I have my life fixed in the Lord; and no matter if I live or die, I know my life is secure in His arms. So, I don't fear death anymore because I know in whom I have trust.

It's true that sometimes can become tedious when I have to deal with all kinds of medications every day, and it becomes over-whelming, but (Jeremiah 29:11) I know that He has plans for me, and I won't leave this earth until He says so. So, I don't worry about tomorrow. I just purpose to keep running the race that He has set for me to run without getting weary in well-doing because in due season, I shall reap what I have sown (Galatians 6:9).

So if you are dealing with any sickness or disease, I encourage you not to give up and to trust in Him that He has your life in His hands, and as long as you are in Him, He won't let you go. So fix your life in Him, and believe me, you won't be disappointed.

Love, forgive, and live for Him. Why did I say forgive? Because when we have any root of bitterness, it manifests in our lives with sickness, stress, and our lives are miserable. Please learn to forgive even though that person doesn't deserve it. When you practice it by saying "I forgive you," you will free yourself from that bondage that kept you in prison. And you will begin to experience that feeling a little bit lighter.

So, I hope this topic has helped you from the bottom of my heart and understand a little bit more of how God wants to work in your life. Peace. Everything is going to be all right and begin that healing now with trust in the Lord. Love you all.

A Call to Your Consciousness

Why, I want you to reflect about the behavior that this world has toward other people, especially with people who have HIV. I have experienced rejection and lots of loneliness because people don't educate themselves and just react by what they fear about it. They might be so picky that they'd rather live their lives, excluding them from their lives. Or if they do have them in their lives, they are afraid of getting sick too when it's just a matter of educating yourself.

Any sickness we deal with, we need to have some kind of education, so we will understand a little bit more and how to treat it. And it amazes me that in 2020, there are a lot of people that don't know how to deal with HIV.

People infected rather not to say anything to their friends or family members because of fear of their reaction. By making this choice, we become isolated from those we really care about. And we have a sense of loneliness, and pain overcomes our lives.

Sometimes deep inside, we yearn for affection and love, and not only that but comprehension. Deep inside, we would like to have someone to share how our last blood test results was and to have someone that would ask us about our health. We need someone in our lives that really cares about how we feel and how we collect our emotions toward death which we deal with every day.

Instead of people that don't understand us, we need people that truly love us and have compassion like Jesus did. And not only with HIV but any other kinds of diseases around the world.

I'm calling you to be understandable and not to be judgmental with other person's circumstances in life but to love. We need more love in this world and compassion, and if that means that you have to read a little bit more about their condition, then do it and show them that you really care about their circumstances. Let them know that you are getting educated and that you care about them. Don't forget that we all need someone that cares about us and deserves to be loved by you.

Ask them how they feel of taking meds every day. How was their last lab? How do they feel about facing death every day? Ask them if they need help with their groceries or at home. Ask them if they know Jesus, so they won't fear death anymore. And show them that you really care. By doing this, you will find that you will take a step to better yourself and others.

Please do it now and see that by caring for others, God will give you a reward in heaven that you will not imagine. Don't forget what the Word says in Matthew 25:35, "For I was hungry and you gave me something to eat, I was thirsty and you gave me something to drink, I was a stranger and you invited me in. As you did to this little ones you have done to me." Let's take Jesus's example to better our lives by doing His will and making others feel loved.

> Blessed are the poor in spirit, for theirs is the king-
> dom of heaven. Blessed are those who mourn, for
> they shall be comforted. Blessed are the meek, for

they shall inherit the earth. Blessed are those who hunger and thirst for righteousness, for they shall be filled. Blessed are the merciful, for they shall obtain mercy. Blessed are the pure in heart, for they shall see God. Blessed are the peacemakers, for they shall be called sons of God. Blessed are those who are persecuted for righteousness's sake. For theirs is the kingdom of heaven. (Matthew 5:3–10)

My viewpoint: I see here how the believer should conduct his life and some of the challenges that we might encounter as we live a life that reflects His character and the blessings that follow.

You are the salt of the earth; but if the salt loses its flavor, how shall it be seasoned? It is then good for nothing but to be thrown out and trampled underfoot by men (Matthew 5:13–16).

My viewpoint: Salt is a very important mineral that we use for cooking. Without the special amount that we put into it, the food it will taste horrible. The way we season the earth according to the Word of God is by sharing what Jesus did for us and bringing someone at His feet.

You are the light of the world. A city that is set on a hill cannot be hidden. Nor do they light a lamp and put it under a basket, but on a lampstand, and it gives light to all who are in the house. Let our light so shine before men, that they may see your good works and glorify your Father in heaven. (Matthew 5:14)

My viewpoint: This passage here is quickening us to be brave as Christians and not to be ashamed of the gospel. If others don't see the light in us, then how are they going to be saved? So, let your light shine on the earth.

Therefore, I say to you, do not worry about your life, what you will eat or what you will drink; nor about your body, what you will put on. Is not life more than food and the body more than clothing? Look at the birds of the air, for they neither sow nor reap nor gather into barns; yet our heavenly Father feeds them. Are you not of more value than they? Which of you by worrying can add one cubit to his stature? So why do you worry about clothing? Consider the lilies of the field, how they grow: they neither toil nor spin; and yet I say to you that even Salomon in all his glory was not arrayed like one of these.

Now if God so clothes the grass of the field, which today is, and tomorrow is thrown into the oven, will He not much more clothe you, O you of little faith? Therefore, do not worry, saying, 'What shall we eat?' or 'What shall we drink?' or 'What shall we wear?' For after all these things the Gentiles seek. For your heavenly Father knows that you need all these things. But seek first the kingdom of God and His righteousness, and all these things shall be added unto you. Therefore, do not worry about tomorrow for tomorrow will worry about its own things. Sufficient for the day is its own trouble. (Matthew 6:25–34)

My viewpoint: I know sometimes, it might be difficult not to worry about our tomorrow, but one thing I learned is that when we pour our lives into God's hands in prayer and learn to trust Him, I know that He will make a way. He certainly does the miracles into our lives. So, pray and you will see an awesome result.

Judge not, that you be not judged. For with what judgment you judge, you will be judged; and with the measure you use, it will be measured back to you. And why do you look at the speck in your brother's eye, but do not consider the plank in your own eye? Or how can you say to your brother, 'Let me remove the speck from your eye'; and look, a plank is in your own eye? Hypocrite! First remove the plank from your own eye, and then you will see clearly to remove the speck from your brother's eye. (Matthew 7:1–6)

My viewpoint: Here, the Scripture is very clear. Check your life first before trying to consider the life of others. And don't forget that if you sow love and understanding, that's what you are going to reap.

A New Commandment I Leave You

In Matthew 22:37, Jesus said to him, "You shall love the Lord your God with all your <u>heart</u> with all your <u>soul</u> and with all your <u>mind</u>. This is the first and great commandment. And the second is like it: You shall love your neighbor as yourself. On these two commandments hand all the law and the prophets."

I don't know where love has gone. Today! Most of the people I know are self-centered; they worry about themselves, and some people don't even care about God. They have gone astray from the truth. That's why I'm putting some Scriptures here and there just in case you have never read the Bible, you will be able to glimpse some of God's Word and learn a little bit about what it says.

I want to share with you that God's love for you is everlasting, and His desire toward you is that you come to Him. He is waiting for you with open arms to reconcile with Him through Jesus Christ. As God has an unconditional love toward you and loves you still knowing the condition you are in, He still desires that you love Him with all your *mind, soul,* and *heart.* He wants you to surrender all that you have and are to Him and love Him the same way He loves you.

God knows that out of the heart flows the issues of life, and He wants to be the center of everything that is in your heart, not because He wants to control you. But if He gives you love, He would want you to love Him the same way. So now I'm going to break down the three things that God wants us to love Him with, so you can have a glimpse of what He expects from you. By the way, I don't consider myself someone that has lots of knowledge, but the little I know of the years that I have been Christian, I will speak.

Heart

First, He warns us to guard our heart because out of it flows the issues of life. He knows that our lives are in danger if we don't make the right decisions, and He warns us to guard it. The consequences of our decisions could be positive or negative, and we have to be careful of every decision we make. Sometimes we let our hearts dictate what we should do without examining if it's the right one. But there is one decision that it's going to be drastically directing the course of our eternity, and only you can make it. Nobody else is entitled to do it for you, and that's who you want to pass eternity with. My purpose is to warn you that there is a heaven and there is a hell, and both of them are drastically good or bad. So, we have to be wise and make the right choice. My purpose with this book is that you will be able to glimpse how good He is been to me and to let you know that there is nothing that can stand in your way when you have the Lord Jesus by your side and to tell you further in this book that there is only one way to heaven—and that is through Jesus.

Soul

The soul controls our feelings; we could feel happy or sad. Our physical bodies are connected with emotions and feelings toward what we encounter in our daily basis. The soul and mind are connected to make decisions, and sometimes we are controlled by the emotions of the soul and we make decisions based on how we feel. So, don't matter how you feel right now—happy, sad, or sick—don't let that control your life. So, we need to learn to control our emotions.

Mind

Your mind will put your soul and your heart into action. In the mind is our intellectual and our battlefield; and believe me, if you have a clear mind, you can do wonders. A mind that is focused can achieve all that the heart and soul desires. So let's focus in the Maker of heaven and earth and let Him work through us, so we can win from now on.

God wants to captivate us with all that we are—*heart, soul,* and *mind* and to love him with all our being because He wants to reward us with all His blessings and to start a fellowship with Him. He will lavish us with an unconditional love, a kind of love that we never have experienced in our lives. It brings great comfort to me just to know that someone higher than me loves me with an everlasting love and that He won't betray me or look down on me, someone that understands me and that I can come to Him in any time. He is there to listen to my cry.

As we learn to love God, He will prepare us to love our neighbor as we love our selves. Then when you see a homeless person, you would want to help them because whatever bad is happening to them, you are feeling their pain. Or if you see someone sick, you will have compassion because the love of God is in your heart. And that love of God put in you will be inclined to help others, and by doing that, we are fulfilling God's Word, not because we are obligated but because God's love has been poured into our hearts.

So, my biggest questions are these now: Do you love the Lord? How intense is your love for Him? Do you think you loved Him just a little bit? Do you love yourself? How great do you love yourself? Do you love your neighbor?

All these questions are very important to reflect now, so God will help you to make the right decision. So, I think we can start with a word of gratitude for all He has done for us, for our lives, family, job, shelter, food, pets, friends, and health. And if you don't think these are valid things to be thankful for, consider the air, water, cars, and all that He allowed us to have. If you don't think He deserves glory for all these things, I do.

Even though I have questions that I can't answer now, but one day He will. I know that life could be frustrating sometimes, and we want answers now. We say this at times, "If God knows this is harmful to me, why does He allow it in my life?" And we rebelled against Him, but if we learn to trust Him (Romans 8:28), He will turn that very bad thing that happened into good; if we don't faint in well doing, for in due season, we shall reap (Galatians 6:9).

So, let's love God with all our heart soul and mind. And love our neighbor as ourselves. And everything shall be added to you. Love! Yes, that's the keyword because perfect love cast away fear (1 John 4:18). So, don't worry if others don't love you back. Just remember, God is the great equalizer, and as we give, we shall receive.

Worship Music

Why did I add this topic to my book? Because I believe that what we put into our ears is directing the course of our lives. If all we listen to are the worldly songs, we will end up into a trap of the enemy. Have you ever heard a song and it gets stuck in your head and all you do is think of that song? That is because there are forces that want to take control of your mind and keep you away from the peace that God brings. Now you will say to me, "Marlyn, you have been super spiritual"? No, I want you to know that there are two forces in this world—evil or good. You have to make your decision if you'll be for Christ or the devil.

You can't be a Christian and be listening to things from this world, or you give your life to the Lord and let the Holy Spirit transform you, or you will be a weak Christian moving away for every wind. Don't forget that 2 Corinthians 3:2–3 says that we are open books read by all. Are we going to give a good testimony of a godly life, or we are going to be fellowshipping with the devil?

"God has called us to holiness" (1 Peter 1:14–16). "We are in the world, but we are not of this world" (John 17:16). And the Word of God says in James 4:4 that if we are friend with the world, we are enemies of God.

There is a passage in the Bible that talks of spirits that distress people, and in this case, it was Saul. It is found in 1 Samuel 16: 14–23. I'm going to tell you a little bit what happened to Saul. There was a distressed spirit that troubled him, and he said, "Let's find a skillful player on the harp."

So, his workers said, "I have seen the son of Jesse, who is skillful in playing, a mighty man of valor, a man of war, prudent in speech, and a handsome person; and the Lord is with him." And every time David played the harp to Saul, he was refreshed and made well, and the spirit would depart from him.

So, you see what happens when we choose to worship the only truth, God? Evil forces go away, and we become free in His presence. One thing I have purpose in my life is not to give head to the things of this world; the TV is full of garbage, and if all you do is watch all of that, you will find yourself weak into the things of God. If you won't find time to read God's Word or to pray because all these things consume you and then you will ask yourself, "Why? Why, don't I understand the Bible?" It's because you haven't taken time to study it or to get a Bible dictionary that will explain a little bit more what was going on in those times.

So please don't tell me that you are experiencing distractions while you are trying to pray or that you get sleepy when you go to church. What happened is that your focus is not there.

"Let's leave aside everything that snares us and let's have some time of worship and prayer" (Hebrews 12:1–2). When we worship, we get into a new realm of the Spirit, and you can be healed, set free, and transformed by the power of God—things that were difficult for you to change will have a breakthrough. The Word of God says in John 4:19–26 that God is looking for worshipers that worship Him in spirit and in truth. When He says in spirit, it means that your whole being is engaged into it and that from your heart, there is not division or fakeness; but everything that flows from you is truth, pure, and absolutely sincere. So, I invite you to find a good worship CD and start to worship with freedom and love to the Lover of our souls. I promise you that you will find yourself in the best place you could ever be, and God will be pleased with you because we were created to worship Him.

Beloved reader, I understand that if you are a newborn Christian, you will have some struggles letting it go. But my advice to you is that you purpose to live for the Lord and try to be devoted to Him who loves your soul. The Holy Spirit will help you all the way through. He is our helper and will never leave you alone through this process. There are some Christian stations. Tune in or buy a worship CD that will help you enter to the throne room of God. Don't forget if God is by our side, who can be against us? So, worship the only One worthy of praise. Jesus Christ our Lord and Savior.

You Are Not Alone

In my case, I felt very lonely through all these years. I had a sense of isolation because of HIV. I thought I was the only one with this disease without realizing I wasn't alone in this situation. When I first found out, I spent more than fifteen years of my life feeling afraid of what others might think or do when I expose them to my reality. And not only that. Raising a child that was HIV negative with all my fears, I'd been told that I have to wash everything (spoons, forks, plates, cups, pans, cloth etc.) with Clorox because the knowledge of it was so little. And not only that but I had been schizophrenic. Paranoia made it very difficult for both of us. It was back in 1995 when I found out. And also, it was a short period of time that I began to suffer a mental illness which made it worse.

But why this topic? Because you are not alone in whatever situation you are in. Diseases come and go, and we all suffer for the reality of death. The separation of loved ones could make us feel depressed. But if you trust in the Lord no matter of the length of days we have on this earth, everything is going to be okay.

I had the opportunity of watching kids of parents with HIV on a camp, and they have so many emotions as they were performing a night of talents. One was anxiety; some were crying, and all those types of emotions they faced, we faced it too. The fact of not knowing what will be next with their loved ones could be scary. There are children, teenagers, and adults that are involved with HIV or with the diseases; and sometimes they don't know how to cope with the pain and sense of rejection, and that is why we have to come out of the shell and break the stigma that this world has and ask them to be more acceptable and compassionate toward those who are suffering. But if we realize that there are millions of people with this condition with the isolation and fear of death and rejection, then we can see of ways we could be a blessing to them...

Outside this world, there are support groups and things you can do to come out of the isolation. Don't let depression and loneliness take control of you. Your life is so valuable, and it's enough with taking meds every day and the pressure of the society that does judges people. But I encourage you to be part of something that makes you feel valuable and wanted. It will bring some sense of worth, and you will feel that you have accomplished something important in your life. Don't let life just pass by but conquer the world with a great attitude. Stop complaining about the pain and aches. The more you complain, the more pain you will have. So, try to overcome the disease with good thinking and believing in God. You and I will overcome until the end. One thing we have to do is to learn how to navigate our lives in whatever situation you are in, not only with HIV but also with schizophrenia as well. We have to unclothe our minds with negativity and think on possibilities of how to better our self and others.

I know that with mental illness, it is a little bit more different because our capacities to process some things could be challenging, but we can do it with God's help. We can do it and be able to achieve everything your mind is set for. You just need to work on getting your mind right. Once your mind is right, you must set goals even though they are little and focus on getting what you want. You can do it. I had this book in my mind since 1997 when I had my crisis and life has hit me hard, but I had that in mind. And no one can talk me out of it until I did it.

One thing I have been doing through all these years is trusting the Lord for my complete healing, but once I knew that the Lord loves me no matter what I have done, it gave me a sense of freedom, and I began to declare the Word of God over my life; and as a consequence of it, I can say He has been faithful.

For thirty years, I had been dealing with HIV without being hospitalized for any opportunistic disease. That is my life tribute to the Lord, a life dedicated to Him, of course with up and downs but with Him. Also, only two crises in my life with schizophrenia. One after the other was when I first found out in twenty-one years, I haven't changed my meds, and I have been taking the same dose of medication. That, in itself, is a miracle! I know how it feels to be confused and depressed and also out of mind, but every time I felt like that, I bow my knees and pray. In other words, cry out to God, and He has delivered me one more time from my confusion.

So, in all of this, the Lord is using my life to be a blessing to others and be able to say yesterday is gone. Today is a brand-new day with expectations of a better future. Just trust in Him, and He will take you through. So, remember, you are not alone.

Right Timing

In Ecclesiastes 3:1–8, it says that there is time for everything:

A time to be born and time to die.
A time to plant and a time to uproot.
A time to kill and a time to heal.
A time to tear down and a time to build.
A time to weep and a time to laugh.
A time to mourn and a time to dance.
A time to scatter stones and a time to gather them.
A time to embrace and a time to refrain from embracing.
A time to search and a time to give up.
A time to keep and a time to throw away.
A time to tear and a time to mend.
A time to be silent and a time to speak.
A time to love and a time to hate.
A time for war and a time for peace.

Now why did I add this topic? Because there is a time for everything, and the fact that you are reading this book right now is because God Almighty has appointed you from the beginning to read through these pages. There is nothing that can escape from the will of God, and He has set on His own timing here and right now for you to read this which has tremendous value to God.

It took me twenty-one years to be exact with you to write this book, and God has been preparing you for such a time as this. Whatever your circumstances are, I want you to know that He is in control and that He cares. God has His own timing for every human that has been on this earth. He didn't just throw every humankind at once on this earth but allowed us to live and die for certain appointed time according to His divine purpose.

In my personal opinion, I believe we are in the last days and the Word of God warned us of the times we are living. One example in the Bible that speak to us to get ready is in Matthew 25:1–13, and it says:

> At that time the Kingdom of heaven will be like ten virgins who took their lamps and went out to meet the bridegroom. Five of them were foolish and five were wise. The foolish ones took their lamps but did not take any oil with them. The wise ones, however, took oil in jars along with their lamps. The bridegroom was a long time in coming, and they all became drowsy and fell asleep. At midnight the cry rang out. "Here's the bridegroom!" Come out to meet him! Then all ten virgins woke up and trimmed their lamps. The foolish ones said to the wise, "Give us some of your oil, our lamps are going out." NO, they replied, there may not be enough for both us and you. Instead, go to those who sell oil and buy some for yourselves. But while they were on their way to buy the oil, the bridegroom arrived. The virgins who were ready went in with him to

the wedding banquet. And the doors were shut. Later the others also came. "Lord, Lord they said open the door for us." But he replied, "Truly I tell you; I don't know you." Therefore, keep watch, because you don't know the day or the hour.

So, I encourage you to get prepared for the bridegroom unless He finds you sleeping and you lose the awesome opportunity to be with Him. Put everything in a balance right now and see what weighs more. And make the Lord the most important thing of your life, so when He comes, we are prepared for His coming.

You are on the right timing. The clock is ticking, and His coming is at hand. Get ready. Get ready. Soon the trumpet will sound, and we will be caught up in the air, and the death in Christ will rise to be with the Lord.

Faith and Medicines

In my walk with the Lord, this topic has been of tremendous challenge. In one way, I want to please God, and in another way, I want to walk in healing. I always thought that if I love the Lord, I have to leave all the medications and walk by faith, but I realized that God is a God of order. He won't ask you to leave all the meds if He hasn't healed you yet.

When I first found out that I was sick with HIV, I was a newborn baby in the Lord—only one year old. And I heard many preaching of faith saying, "Throw your meds to the garbage and walk by faith." And I did many times in my attempt to please God but never went to the doctors to confirm it. So, I ended up with low T cells and more crazy then I was. And this kept happening for many years with the struggle of faith and the fact that I have to take the medications. In my love for the Lord, I wanted to please Him, but the struggle was still there.

I knew that Word of God says that by Your stripes, you were healed, and I began to confess it through all these years. And I believe that is what has kept me well for thirty years. But after living with all these diseases all these years and confessing the Word of God, I realize something very interesting. Are you ready to find out?

I realize that I can use the same faith without medications or with medications and leave everything in God's hands because He is the One that has the ultimate Word. Our part is to believe in His Word and confess it over our lives, and the rest is up to Him. And if you have been to a church and believe that you are healed, go to the doctor for confirmation because God does things in order. So, in due time, you can give Him all the glory.

So, this is my discovery. Take your meds and believe God for a healing, and in due season, He will manifest strong in your life.

Let's Dream Together

Have you ever been to a wedding? The Lord says in His Word that we are His bride and that one day, we will be marrying Jesus. He is the bridegroom. I have been in a wedding that has been stunningly beautiful. People on this earth take time to prepare their wedding very seriously. They have a period of preparation, making sure that everything is going to be perfect. The reception, tables, food, entertainment, flowers, dress, makeup, perfume, shoes, priest, church, etc.

We, as brides, should be getting ready for that day. We need to be in tune with the Lord, so it doesn't take us by surprise and lose the opportunity to be meeting the bridegroom face-to-face. We are ought to prefer Jesus before anything else in this life. He is the hidden treasure that we all want. He will fill the thirst that we all have in our soul, and one day soon, we will experience this wedding. The bridegroom is taking care of everything in heaven for us right now. What a precious day it will be.

Can you imagine all the angels with harps and trumpets announcing the entrance of the bride, and we with white cloths receiving Jesus in all His splendor and God Himself performing the wedding ceremony? What an awesome moment just to be there with the Lover of our souls. I can't glimpse the splendor and majesty of Jesus. Can you agree with me that it's a privilege to just be part of His bride? Don't take it lightly. He loves us so much that He is making all the arrangements for that day. Would you come to Him today and say, "Lord, I want to be part of that bride that will be yours forever"?

If we, in our humanity, can feel His presence just in a few minutes that the Holy Spirit allows us to have, can you imagine just to be with Him? I believe that His presence will be so thick in our lives that we will want to bow down before him forever. He will make us perfect; there are no imperfections in heaven.

You see the sky and you wonder if there is heaven and how it is. The enemy wants to blind your lives with unbelief. I encourage you to read in the Bible the book of Revelation 4 where it says what's going on in heaven right now and its worship to the Almighty God and to Jesus. The work of Holy Spirit right now is to convince you that you will be there with Him forever if you choose to believe in Jesus. How serious are you going to take that wedding with the Lover of our soul?

In Awe of Him

Every time I think in God's power, it leaves me in awe. Just to see the trees, the earth, the ocean, the sky, the animals, the humanity, and all His creation. How He can make flowers with all different colors and different shapes and the trees with all their strength, some shorter or taller wider or thinner? What about the earth where God has given the human wisdom to build houses, buildings, roads, and the ocean so vast and beautiful, the sky where He dwells, the sun, the moon, the universe, and all the precious stars that we see? Have you ever taken time to look up at night where the sky is full of stars? How beautiful, right? If we just try to meditate in these things, I get in awe just to imagine God Himself who is the Creator of everything that exist and made the rain, the snow, and the humankind.

How, by a little sperm, God makes us alive in our mother's womb? And since He gives us life, He knows us and loved us from that moment that we were in her womb. In Isaiah 49:1, it says,

"Listen to me, all of you in far-off lands! The Lord called me before my birth; from within the womb he called me by name."

He not only made you but called you by name. What an intimate God He is. So, do you know that your life hasn't taken God by surprise, or do you think that He doesn't know what's going on in your life right now? He made you. He knows you intimately; you might not know Him now, but He does know you, and all that He wants is to have a reconciliation with you as sons and as daughters. But a holy God can't tolerate sin. That's why He sent Jesus to die and shed his blood for you and me. So why this reconciliation with Jesus? Because if you decide to accept the sacrifice for your sins, your relationship with the One who made you will begin again. God who is holy decided to choose you today as you read this book and wants to have part in your life because He loves you and wants fellowship with you.

So, you might be asking yourself, "Why me? I'm wicked. I don't deserve Him." But let me tell you that His love is extended to you too. I was wicked, once separated from His sight, and He chose in His love to love me. He didn't die for the just only but for that those who were lost without him. So, make a decision for Jesus today as you read!

So, it struck me in awe the awesome love of God. In Philippians 2:5, it says:

> Let this mind be in you which was also in Christ Jesus, who, being in the form of God did not consider it robbery to be equal with God, but made Himself of no reputation, taking the form of a bondservant, and coming in the likeness of men. And being form in appearance as man, He humbled Himself and became obedient to the point of death even death of the cross. Therefore God also has highly exalted Him and given Him the name which is above every name, that at the name of Jesus every knee should bow, and of those in heaven, and of those on earth, and

of those under the earth and that every tongue should confess that Jesus Christ is Lord, to the glory of God the Father.

Wow, it leaves me breathless every time I read this. So, because of the miracle that took place in Mary's life and now in our lives, because of that, we can rejoice. The day of salvation has come to our lives. Today I praise the Lord for all of you who are going to make a decision for Jesus Christ.

A CALL FROM THE LORD

Let's see what the Spirit of the LORD says. I'm calling from the north to the south, from the east to the west. Everyone is invited to the call from God. Listen what the Lord wants to say. Don't wait. The day of salvation is today. Make Jesus the Lord of your life and you will see me face-to-face if you keep running the race that is set before you. I will break the strongholds of unbelief in you and your family. Just trust in me, and you will become brand-new. Please decide to give your lives to Jesus, and if you haven't done this, repeat with me now the prayer for salvation.

Dear Lord Jesus,

I come to you today with a repented heart, knowing that I have sinned, and I'm recognizing the sacrifice that you did for me at the cross in Calvary. I repent, Lord Jesus. Forgive my sins and wash me with your precious blood, so I will be made whole. Please, Lord, come to live inside of me. Today I open the door of my heart, and I proclaim You Lord of my life. Please write my name in the book of life and fill me with Your Holy Spirit, so I will be with You. Now I'm yours. Thank You, Jesus, for your grace and love. Amen.

Now I am going to pray for you.

Dear Father, now that they have been reconciled with you through the blood of Jesus, I ask You that You will give them wisdom to make right choices in life and that they will learn to surrender everything to You. Protect them from evil and heal their broken hearts as they come to You. Holy Spirit, I thank you for the transformation that You will begin in their lives from this day forward. And, Lord, if they are sick, heal them for the glory of Your name. Thank You, Lord, because I know you heard my prayers. In Jesus's name. Amen

Now that you have made the most important decision in your life, I encourage you to go to a church where the name of Jesus is exalted. When you go, don't look at people because we are all with imperfections, but keep your eyes in Jesus. Every time you go, purpose in your heart to go to a church and say, "Jesus, I come to worship You and Holy Spirit. Put love in me, so I can love and understand my brothers and sisters. Ask Him to unify us as You and the Father are one."

Every time you go to church, go with the expectation to have a visitation from the Lord in your heart. I just want to tell you that I'm proud of you. Until then, let's fight the good fight. Amen.

Conclusion

In conclusion, I want to thank you for picking up this book and letting me minister to you my experiences mixed with my belief in the Lord Jesus Christ. I thank you for allowing the Word of God to speak to your heart and be open to it even if you are not a believer.

My hope is that this world will be more loving and compassionate with everyone that are struggling with any kind of disease. I want the world to know that we need you and that with unity in love, we will be able to conquer any disease that might come our way.

And my biggest wish above all is that you have given life to *Jesus*, so no matter if it's now or in eternity, I will be able to see you and know the impact that this book made in your life.

With love,
Marlyn Torres

ABOUT THE AUTHOR

My life basically was kind of isolated but when I saw that I could work a little bit I started as a caregiver for autistic young adults. Then I found another job as a job coach, training young adults with disabilities to succeed in their work force. Then I volunteer at the relief bus helping homeless with food, clothing and info. Also how to get different resources to ease their life journey. Then I volunteer as Pastoral care giver at a local hospital then life hit me hard and I isolate myself for a few years living from the government, but still contribute to the community helping a teacher with crafts for seniors. Now I'm working as a home health aid and volunteering in a nursing home giving bible studies to seniors that lived there. My life it's been mostly all the time volunteering but what really matters is the fulfillment those has brought into my life.

CPSIA information can be obtained
at www.ICGtesting.com
Printed in the USA
LVHW110426030221
678219LV00007B/673